BRANDING FOR SUCCESS

YOLAN WALLACE

BRANDING FOR SUCCESS

A GUIDE TO BUILDING A STRONG FOUNDATION FOR YOUR COMPANY

Charleston, SC
www.PalmettoPublishing.com

*BRANDING FOR SUCCESS: A guide to building
a strong foundation for your company.*

First Edition

Paperback ISBN: 978-1-64990-366-2

WELCOME

Welcome to the Product Launch Accelerated Program! Your journey to becoming one of the world's leading entrepreneurs begins here. Take a moment and let that soak in. You may be excited, scared, anxious, curious, or skeptical but, I want you to know that all these feelings are what's going to make you the best entrepreneur.

Because you are here, it is fair to assume that:

1. You are capable of creating a 'Banging Brand.'
2. Your product or service is very marketable.
3. You have a skill or idea that you want to create structure around.
4. You are coachable, and willing to go the extra mile for your dream.
5. You want to build a successful brand that will impact your financial situation.

Congratulations! You are already off to a great start. Let's begin!

BRANDING AS A FOUNDATION

WHAT IS A BRAND?

QUESTIONS TO ASK

YOURSELF

- Do people automatically want to tell a friend about their experience?
- Do they freely repost my images and content?
- Do customers get excited over my packaging?
- Do people tell me they love my logo or theme?

Along your journey, whether you purchased an item or scrolled across a product or service on the internet, you can attest that 'Presentation is Key'. Those eye-catching ads, logos, color coded IG pages and individuals who dress the part, all make you want whatever it is they are selling. My goal for this book is that whatever you are selling, people will automatically want.

Let us take a moment to first define what a brand is. It is a name, term, design, symbol, or any other feature that identifies one seller's goods or services as distinct from those of other sellers.

Visually, your brand should begin to evoke feelings in your potential customers. You will often hear customers say things such as, "Oh my gosh, it looks like it tastes really good" or, "I just know that feels good," etc. Customers should be proud to display your packaging or product and want to share their wonderful experience, thus, referring new customers to you.

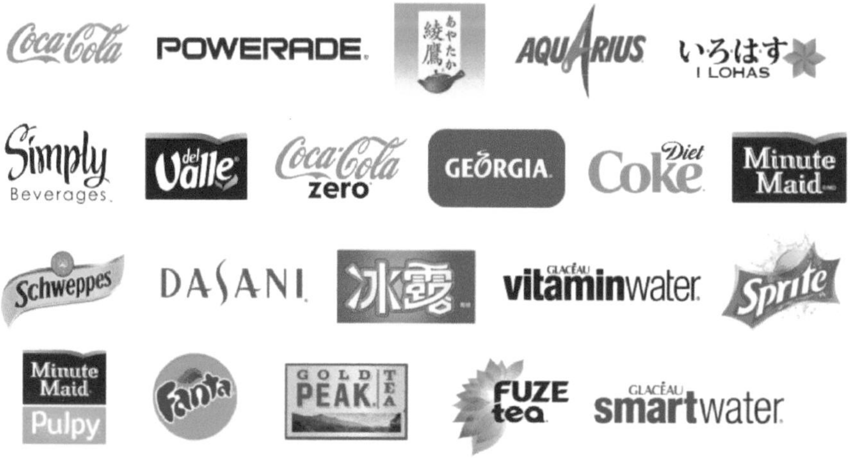
Coca-Cola
POWERADE
綾鷹
あやたか
AQUARIUS
いろはす
I LOHAS
Simply
Beverages
del Valle
Coca-Cola
zero
GEORGIA
Diet
Coke
Minute Maid
Schweppes
DASANI
冰露
GLACÉAU
vitaminwater
Sprite
Minute Maid
Pulpy
Fanta
GOLD PEAK TEA
FUZE tea
GLACÉAU
smartwater

Caption

Branding is one of the most important aspects of any business: large or small. A brand strategy sets you apart from your competitors. Your brand starts with you: How are you presenting yourself to the public, to friends, and to family? The way you operate your business, customers will mimic you. For example, if you are always late, how will you expect your customer to pay you on time?

When you think about your brand, think about the entire experience your customers will have. Branding doesn't happen overnight; it's a well thought out strategic plan. The Product Launch Accelerated Program was designed to give your company the leading edge on launch day with the branding associated with your company.

Throughout this program, my team and I will ensure that your brand is a recurring theme throughout, and it begins with **YOU**. Getting the necessary coaching to transition from a worker mindset to a Business Owner, and then to an Entrepreneur, is very important as you are now navigating new territory.

A brand is more than the physical components of your business. A brand includes physical components such as: logo, website, domain, and colour theme, but is not limited to these.

Why Does Your Business Need a Brand?

What exactly makes up a brand? A brand identity consists of:

1. Brand Elements
2. Brand Promise
3. Brand Communications

4. Brand Expectations
5. Brand Persona

Top Reasons Why Your Business Needs a Brand

Your brand tells people about your business. Your full brand experience from the visual elements such as logo, color scheme, Thank You cards, invoices, customer service etc. tells your customer about your company. Is your business inviting? Do you create a space where customers can express themselves respectfully regarding the way they feel about their experience whether good or bad?

Branding Promotes Recognition. If your brand is easily recognized it will create trust when customers are purchasing your products/services. People often do business with companies they are familiar with. Your brand will set you apart from your competitors. How can customers easily recognize your brand from the thousands of similar businesses in the market?

An effective brand generates referrals. People in general love to tell others about their experience. For example, you watched a movie at the cinema and loved every minute of it. You then begin to share your experience with your friends by giving them a long list of reasons why they should go and see the movie. Did the theatre pay you for the promotion? No, they did not; however, because of your wonderful experience, you can't help but share.

A strong brand helps customers know what to expect. Consistency is key! A brand that is consistent with quality products/services will set the level of expectation in customers' minds on how their experience will be each and every time.

CHOOSING A BRAND NAME

CHOOSING A BRAND NAME

The name you choose to represent your brand is the most important element of your brand. In this section, follow the guidelines to creating the perfect brand name.

Types of Brand Names

Here are a few types of brand names that I think will help you to create your brand name from scratch:

- **Initialism:** A name made of initials such as USPS or IBM

- **Neologism:** Completely made-up words, such as Wii or Haagen-Dazs.

- **Founders Names:** Using the names of real people, (especially a founders name), such as Disney.

- **Evocative:** Names that evoke a relevant vivid image, such as Nike or Amazon.

- **Punny:** Some brands create their names from myths, such as Nike.

- **Combination:** Combining multiple words together to create one, such as Microsoft (micro-computer and software).

- **Descriptive:** Names that describe a product/service benefit or function, such as Product Launch Accelerated or Whole Foods.

- **Alliteration and Rhyme:** Names that are fun to say and stick in mind, such as Reese's Pieces or Dunkin' Donuts.

Activity

Make a list of all the possible words you can think of that will describe your business. Use a dictionary or google to find synonyms for each word.

TOP WORDS	SYNONYMS

Make a list of the feelings you want your customers to have when they see, feel, smell or taste your products/services.

TOP WORDS	SYNONYMS

Mix and match your 'top words' with your customer's 'feelings' and the 'synonyms' you found, to create your brand name!

Write below your favorite brand names that you came up with:

_____

_____

_____

_____

_____

How to tell if your brand's name is a good name

- **Meaningful**

  – It communicates your brand essence, conjures an image, and cultivate a positive emotional connection.

- **Distinctive**

  – It is unique, memorable, and stands out from your competitors

- **Accessible**

  – People can easily interpret it, say it, spell it or google it.

- **Protectable**

  – You can trademark it, get the domain, and "own" it legally.

- **Not Limiting**

  – The name should be able to grow with the company, maintain relevance and adaptable to different products and brand extensions.

- **Visual**

  – You can translate/communicate it through design, including icons, logos, colors, etc.

Now that you've gone through the exercises, what name did you choose as your final name? Write it below.

Company Name:_____

I am so excited for you! When you say the name, how does it make you feel? Write down words that describe how you feel.

1. _____

2. _____

3. _____

4. _____

5. _____

6. _____

If you chose words such as excited, scared, calm, speechless, or nervous, then you are on the right path. The name of your company should evoke emotions aligning with your goals. For example, being scared or nervous means your goal is not too small. You may be aware of the saying, "If your goals/dreams don't scare you, they are not big enough." Congratulations on making it this far.

I know it was not easy to dig this deep for a name, but I promise you that taking the time to build the foundation of your business will later give you extreme confidence when talking about your brand.

Now that you've chosen a name, there are some important things to do in order to protect your brand. You could pause and do these now, or you could wait and complete this book, and then attempt them later. Keep in mind that some or all may apply, it just depends on the kind of business or product you are launching.

LEGALITES

PROTECTING YOUR BRAND'S NAME

There are various ways to protect your brand's name. Please bear in mind that some or all listed below may or may not apply.

- First, **Register** the name of your business (for information on how to register, visit your country's government website).

- **Social Media Handle.** Create pages for all social media handles that you will be using. For example, Facebook, Instagram, YouTube, Google+ etc.

- **Trademark** (protect your logo or symbols attached to your brand) visit your government's website.

- **Website**. If you plan to sell your products via a website, secure a domain name by visiting GoDaddy, Wix, Squarespace or any other domain provider of your choice.

TYPES OF BUSINESS STRUCTURE

There are four main types of business structures: Sole Proprietorship, Corporation and Limited Liability Company. These can sometimes be hard to understand, so before choosing if you feel the need to get more clarity, please contact a lawyer or your government website for more information.

Definition

1. Sole Proprietorship

- A sole proprietorship, also known as the sole trader, individual entrepreneurship or proprietorship, is the type of enterprise that is owned and run by one person... and in which there is no legal distinction between the owner and the business entity.

2. Partnership

- A partnership is an arrangement between two or more people to oversee business operations and share its profits and liabilities. In a general partnership company, all members share both profits and liabilities. Professionals like doctors and lawyers often form a limited liability partnership.

3. Corporation
 - A company or group of people authorized to act as a single entity (legally a person) and recognized as such.

4. Limited Liability
 - Limited Liability is a legal status where a person's financial liability is limited to a fixed sum, most commonly the value of a person's investment in a company or partnership. If a company with limited liability is sued, then the claimants are suing the company, not its owners or investors.

DESIGN YOUR LOGO

HOW TO CREATE LOGO

1. Your logo should communicate your brand essence, and cultivate a positive emotional connection.
2. Simple. These logos are the ones people can recognize as soon as they see them.
3. Scalable. A great logo should be simple enough to be able to be scaled down or up and still look good.
4. Memorable/Impactful.
5. Versatile.
6. Relevant.

Write/Draw below ideas for your logo.

Color Scheme

Choosing a color scheme is very important. This should be used throughout your social media handles, website, and product line.

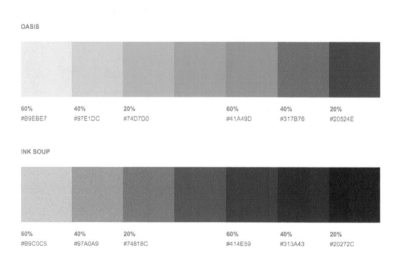

OASIS

| 60% | 40% | 20% | | 60% | 40% | 20% |
| #B9EBE7 | #97E1DC | #74D7D0 | | #41A49D | #317B76 | #20524E |

INK SOUP

| 60% | 40% | 20% | | 60% | 40% | 20% |
| #B9C0C5 | #97A0A9 | #74818C | | #414E59 | #313A43 | #20272C |

Here is a color scheme template. (insert pic below)

If you need help choosing colors go to <u>canvas. com</u>. Search for sample palettes, or even create your own. Each color is associated with a specific code which could be made up of all numbers or numbers and letters. Please ensure that you save this code. To create your logo, you will need to let the person creating the logo know the exact colour. This will save you both time and money on revisions.

What specific colors (exact shade) did you decide on. List them below:

COLOR	COLOR CODE/ HEX CODE

Font Type

Your 'Font Type' should be consistent throughout your brand. This communicates consistency and builds trust. Your font type should be easily understood, legible and easy to scale up or down.

Select from the chart below the font style that stand out to you.

Abadi MT Condensed Light
Albertus Extra Bold
Albertus Medium
Antique Olive
Arial
Arial Black
Arial MT
Arial Narrow
BAZOOKA
Book Antiqua
Bookman Old Style
Boulder
Calisto MT
Calligrapher
Century Gothic
Century Schoolbook
Cezanne
CG Omega
CG Times
CHARLESWORTH
Chaucer
Clarendon Condensed
Comic Sans MS
COPPERPLATE GOTHIC BOLD
COPPERPLATE GOTHIC LIGHT

Allegro
Amazone BT
AmerType Md BT
Arrus BT
Aurora Cn BT
AvantGarde Bk BT
AvantGarde Md BT
BANKGOTHIC MD BT
Benguiat Bk BT
BernhardFashion BT
BernhardMod BT
BinnerD
BREMEN BD BT
CaslonOpnface BT
Charter Bd BT
Charter BT
ChelthmITC Bk BT
CloisterBlack BT
COPPERPLGOTH BD BT
English 111 Vivace BT
ENGRAVERSGOTHIC BT
Exotc350 Bd BT
Freefrm721 Blk BT
FrnkGothITC Bk BT

Write below the font/fonts that stands out:

1. _____

2. _____

If you will be using both, choose one as your main font. Whether you use one or both, be consistent.

Create Your Logo

Create your final logo by adding all the design elements discussed in this chapter.

1. Symbols
2. Color schemes
3. Font

FIRST DRAFT/OPTION 1

SECOND DRAFT/OPTION 2

FINAL DRAFT/OPTION 3

BRAND
BACKGROUND

BRAND BACKGROUND

Knowing your brand's background is paramount. This could make the difference in you getting a million dollar deal or sales on a regular day. You should know your brand's audience and should be able to answer these questions if woken from your sleep.

Brand questionnaire

Answer the questions below. I recommend you study this section as you will need to communicate some if not all when speaking to potential customers or investors.

1. What is your Brand name?

_____

2. What category does your business fall under? (**Service**- provides intangible products, for example, professional skills, expertise, advice, and other similar products.) **Merchandize**- this type of business buys products at wholesale price and sells the same at retail price. They are known as "buy and sell" businesses. **Manufacturing**- a manufacturing business buys products with the intention of using them as materials in making a new product).

_____

3. Why did you start your brand?

_____

_____

_____

_____

_____

_____

4. What general impression do you want to leave with your customer?

_____

_____

_____

_____

_____

5. What makes your business stand out from others in the same field?

_____

_____

_____

_____

_____

6. What will you be selling? (If you've started already, what products are you selling?)

_____

_____

_____

_____

_____

7. What problem does your brand or product solve?

_____

_____

_____

_____

_____

8. Why should someone buy from you?

_____

_____

_____

_____

_____

9. Who is your target audience? (age, income level, hobbies, etc)

_____

_____

_____

_____

_____

_____

10. Describe the unique values your main product/service add to your client.

____

____

____

____

BRAND MISSION STATEMENT

DEFINITION: A mission statement is a short statement of why an organization exists, what its overall goal is, identifying the goal of its operation: what kind of product or service it provides, its primary customers or market, and its geographical region of operation.

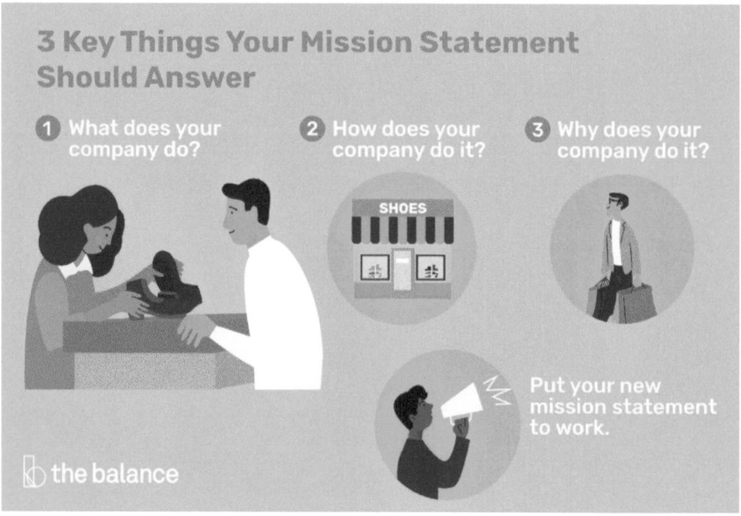
3 Key Things Your Mission Statement Should Answer
1 What does your company do?
2 How does your company do it?
3 Why does your company do it?
SHOES
Put your new mission statement to work.
the balance

With the definition in mind, use information from the Brand Questionnaire to help you write the Mission Statement below.

____

____

____

____

____

____

____

Vision Statement

Definition: A vision statement is an inspirational statement of an idealistic emotional future of a company. Write below where you see the company in the future.

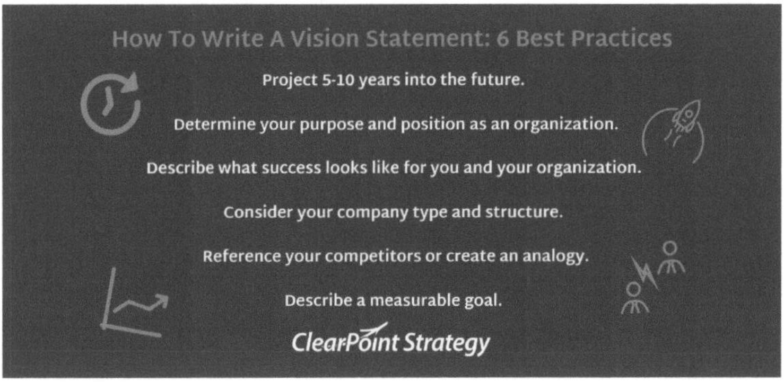
How To Write A Vision Statement: 6 Best Practices
Project 5-10 years into the future.
Determine your purpose and position as an organization.
Describe what success looks like for you and your organization.
Consider your company type and structure.
Reference your competitors or create an analogy.
Describe a measurable goal.
ClearPoint Strategy

Vision Statement

_____

_____

_____

_____

_____

Brand Slogan

Definition: A brand slogan is a small set of words or a short phrase that a business uses to make its company and products stick in the minds of its customers. For example, McDonald-I'm Loving It; Nike-Just Do it; Apple-Think Different; Burger King-Have it Your Way.

Write your slogan below.

_____

_____

_____

_____

_____

Congratulations, you have now built a strong foundation for your company. I look forward to seeing your brand in stores, on television and finally, in my home.

You have successfully completed the Product Launch Accelerated 'Branding Program'!

CPSIA information can be obtained
at www.ICGtesting.com
Printed in the USA
BVHW060125070421
604335BV00012B/282